What Has an 8,000-Pound Tongue and Sings?

Uncover & Discover

WRITTEN BY **Robert Kanner**
ILLUSTRATED BY **Russ Daff**

dingles&company New Jersey

FOR Tg, THE OLDEST SOUL I KNOW

© 2008 dingles & company

ALL RIGHTS RESERVED
No part of this book may be reproduced in any form without written permission from the publishers, except by a reviewer who may quote brief passages in a review to be printed in a newspaper or magazine.

First Printing

Published by dingles & company
P.O. Box 508
Sea Girt, New Jersey 08750

LIBRARY OF CONGRESS CATALOG CARD NUMBER
207903690

ISBN
978-1-59646-780-4

Printed in the United States of America

The Uncover & Discover series is based on the original concept of Judy Mazzeo Zocchi.

ART DIRECTION & DESIGN
Rizco Design

EDITORIAL CONSULTANTS
Andrea Curley

PROJECT MANAGER
Lisa Aldorasi

EDUCATIONAL CONSULTANTS
Melissa Oster and Margaret Bergin

CREATIVE DIRECTOR
Barbie Lambert

PRE-PRESS
Pixel Graphics

WEBSITE
www.dingles.com

E-MAIL
info@dingles.com

5/11

p.b.

Date Due

7.24.11			
1.18.13			
4.15.13			
7.25.19			

SHAMROCK PUBLIC LIBRARY

The **Uncover & Discover** series encourages children to inquire, investigate, and use their imagination in an interactive and entertaining manner. This series helps to sharpen their powers of observation, improve reading and writing skills, and apply knowledge across the curriculum.

Uncover each one and see you can when you're

clue one by
what mammal
discover
done!

The **top of my head** is flat, U-shaped, and almost one-quarter the size of my body.

WHERE IS THE **TOP OF THE HEAD**?

Although I live in the water, I breathe air by using two holes in the top of my head called **blowholes**.

LOOK FOR THE **BLOWHOLES**.

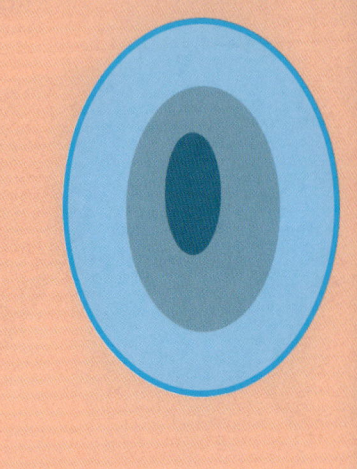
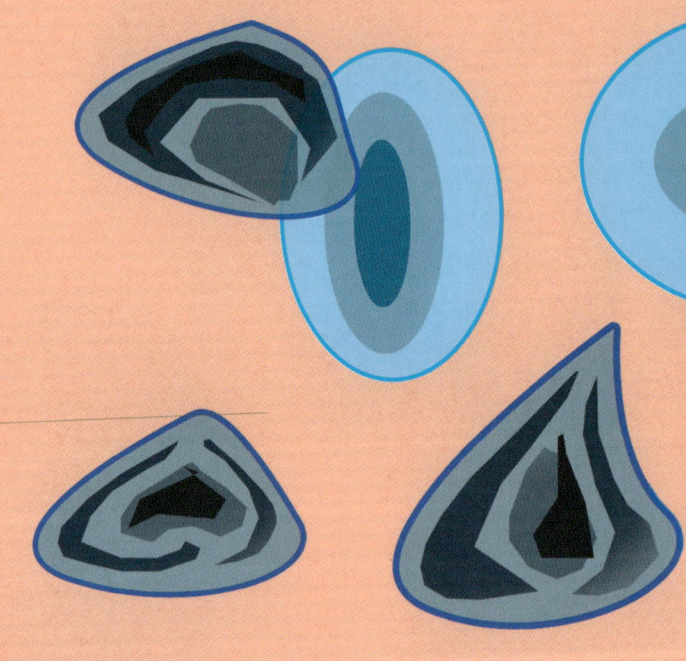
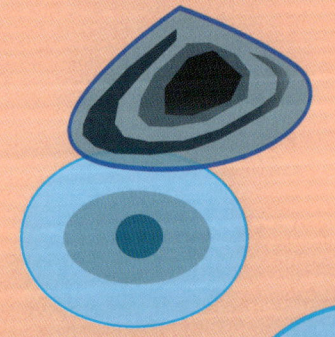

My grapefruit-sized **eyes** are covered by a layer of oil to protect them.

FIND THE EYE.

My long, streamlined **body** lets me swim swiftly through the water.

DO YOU SEE THE **BODY**?

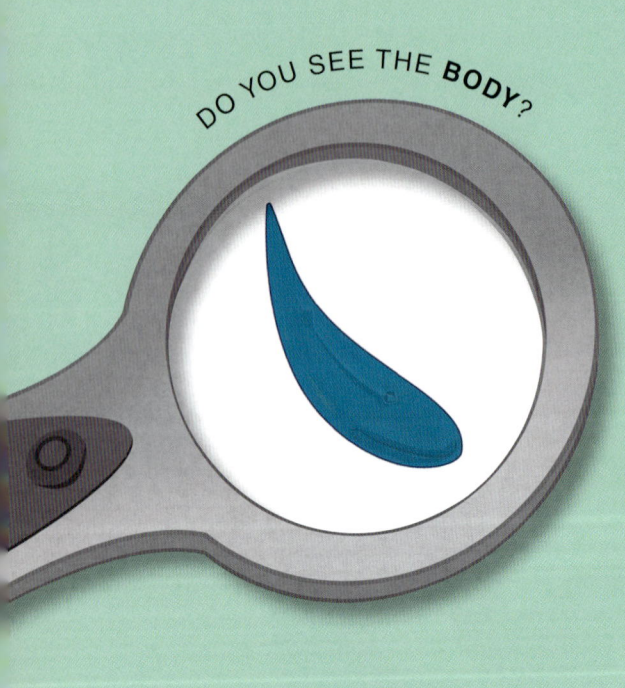
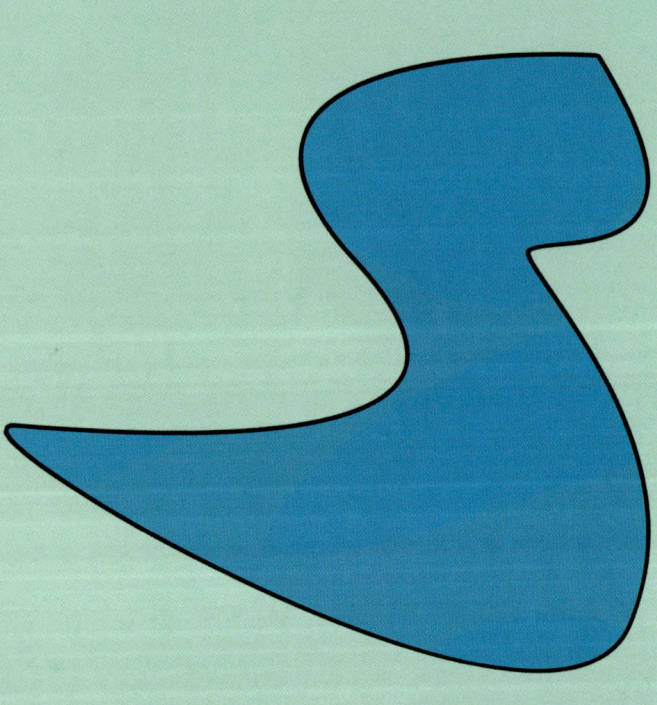

A small, triangular-shaped **dorsal fin** on my back keeps me from tipping over in the water.

WHERE IS THE **DORSAL FIN?**

On each end of my powerful tail are two flat, horizontal fins called **flukes** that move up and down when I swim.

LOOK FOR THE FLUKES.

I use my long, thin **flippers** to change directions in the water.

FIND THE **FLIPPER**.

My **underbelly** has a yellowish tinge because algae, which are tiny plants that grow in the water, stick to it.

DO YOU SEE THE **UNDERBELLY?**

When I eat, I open my large **mouth** and swallow huge amounts of tiny fish called krill.

WHERE IS THE **MOUTH**?

My throat is small but can open really wide when I gulp in ocean water and food, because the **throat grooves** under my chin stretch.

LOOK FOR THE **THROAT GROOVES**.

Instead of teeth I have long, stiff, hairlike material called **baleen plates** that trap krill when the ocean water rushes out of my mouth.

FIND THE BALEEN PLATES.

My 8,000 pound **tongue** licks off the food that gets trapped in my baleen plates.

DO YOU SEE THE **TONGUE?**

You have uncovered the clues. **Have you guessed what I am?**

If not, here are more clues.

1. I am the largest animal on earth.

2. My average size is 70 to 90 feet long (that's about the length of three school buses!).

3. I can weigh between 100 and 150 tons (another way to say this is between 200,000 and 300,000 pounds).

4. I can live for 60 to 70 years.

5. Although I live in the ocean, I am not a fish. I am a mammal. I breathe air, I am warm blooded (which means that my inside body temperature stays about the same even though the temperature outside my body changes), and when I was born, my mother nursed me.

6. I stayed with my mother for 7 to 8 months before I was able to live on my own.

7. I eat mainly krill, which are small shrimplike creatures.

8. I sing songs to communicate. When others hear my song, they repeat what they hear and then add their own sound to it. We do this sometimes for hours or even days at a time.

Now add them up and you'll see...

Do you want to know more about me? Here are some Blue Whale fun facts.

1. A blue whale's heart is as large as a small car.

2. A blue whale has a thick layer of fat under its skin, which helps keep it warm in cold ocean water.

3. A blue whale is one of the loudest animals on earth—even louder than a jet engine. The long, low sounds that it makes can travel for hundreds of miles underwater.

4. Blue whales can be found in all the oceans of the world.

5. A blue whale spends more time in the colder waters, where food is more plentiful. When winter comes and the water gets too cold, the blue whale migrates to warmer waters.

6. Blue whales live alone or swim in small groups. They are frequently seen swimming in pairs.

7. Blue whales are endangered because they were hunted for their meat for many years. Experts estimate that there are fewer than 15,000 blue whales in the ocean today.

Who, What, Where, When, Why, and How

USE THE QUESTIONS who, what, where, when, why, and how to help the child apply knowledge and process the information in the book. Encourage him or her to investigate, inquire, and imagine.

In the Book...

DO YOU KNOW WHO nurses a baby blue whale until it can live on its own?

DO YOU KNOW WHAT the featured mammal in the book is?

DO YOU KNOW WHERE blue whales live?

DO YOU KNOW WHEN blue whales migrate?

DO YOU KNOW WHY blue whales have a thick layer of fat under their skin?

DO YOU KNOW HOW long a blue whale can live?

In Your Life...

Blue whales eat krill. What kind of seafood have you tried?

CROSS-CURRICULAR EXTENSIONS

Math

There are 5 blue whales swimming in the Indian Ocean. Of these, 2 whales weigh 150 tons each. The other 3 whales weigh 90 tons each. How much would the whales weigh all together?

Science

Many years ago, before blue whales were protected by laws, people used to hunt them. Do some research on how blue whales were hunted.

Social Studies

Can you name all the oceans in the world?

Fun Activity

You have uncovered the clues and discovered a blue whale. Unfortunately, there aren't many blue whales left in the world, making these mammals an endangered species. Imagine that there is an Adopt-a-Whale Program at your school. It costs $19 to adopt a whale. You really want to adopt one, but you need to come up with the money to do it.

ASSIGNMENT
Make a list of your ideas.

IMAGINE
Who are you going to ask to help you?
What are you going to do to raise the money?
Where are you going to look for more information?
When do you want to raise the money by?
Why do you want to adopt a whale?
How many whales do you want to adopt?

WRITE
Enjoy the writing process while you take what you have imagined to create your list.

Author

Robert Kanner is part of the writing team for the Uncover & Discover series as well as the Global Adventures and Holiday Happenings series. An extensive career in the film and television business includes work as a film acquisition executive at the Walt Disney Company, a story editor for a children's television series, and an independent family-film producer. He holds a bachelor's degree in psychology from the University of Buffalo and lives in the Hollywood Hills, California, with Tom and Miss Murphy May.

Illustrator

Since graduating from Falmouth School of Art in 1993, **Russ Daff** has enjoyed a varied career. For eight years he worked on numerous projects in the computer games industry, producing titles for Sony PlayStation and PC formats. While designing a wide range of characters and environments for these games, he developed a strong sense of visual impact that he later utilized in his illustration and comic work. Russ now concentrates on his illustration and cartooning full-time. When he is not working, he enjoys painting, writing cartoon stories, and playing bass guitar. He lives in Cambridge, England.